Henry Edward Manning

The grounds of faith

four lectures delivered in St. George's Church

Henry Edward Manning

The grounds of faith
four lectures delivered in St. George's Church

ISBN/EAN: 9783741156441

Manufactured in Europe, USA, Canada, Australia, Japa

Cover: Foto ©Lupo / pixelio.de

Manufactured and distributed by brebook publishing software (www.brebook.com)

Henry Edward Manning

The grounds of faith

The Grounds of Faith.

FOUR LECTURES

DELIVERED IN

ST. GEORGE'S CHURCH, SOUTHWARK

BY

HENRY EDWARD MANNING.

BALTIMORE:
PUBLISHED BY KELLY & PIET,
No. 174 BALTIMORE STREET,
1868.

PUBLISHED WITH THE APPROBATION OF THE MOST
REVEREND ARCHBISHOP.

CONTENTS.

LECTURE I.
REVEALED TRUTH DEFINITE AND CERTAIN........................... 5

LECTURE II.
THE CHURCH A HISTORICAL WITNESS................................. 26

LECTURE III.
THE CHURCH A DIVINE WITNESS....................................... 43

LECTURE IV.
RATIONALISM THE LEGITIMATE CONSEQUENCE OF PRIVATE JUDGMENT... 67

LECTURE I.

REVEALED TRUTH DEFINITE AND CERTAIN

St. John xvii. 3.

"This is life everlasting, that they may know Thee, the only true God, and Jesus Christ whom Thou hast sent."

My purpose is to speak of the grounds of Faith; I do not mean of the special doctrines of the Catholic theology, but of the grounds or foundation upon which all Faith rests.

This is a subject difficult to treat: partly, because it is of a dry and preliminary nature; and partly, because it is not easy to touch upon a matter so long controverted, without treating it likewise in a controversial tone. But I should think it a dishonor to the sacredness of truth itself, if I could treat a matter so sacred and so necessary in a tone of mere argument. I desire to speak, then, for the honor of our Lord, and, if God so will, for the help of those who seek the truth. To lay broad and sure the foundations on which we believe is necessary at all times, because as the end of man is life eternal, and as the means to that end is the knowledge of God, and of Jesus Christ whom He hath sent, our whole being, moral, intellectual, and spiritual demands that we should rightly know, and by knowledge be united with, the mind and will of God. And what is necessary at all times is especially so at this. For this land, once full of light, once united to the great commonwealth of Christendom, and grafted into the mystical vine, through whose every branch and spray life and truth circulate, three hundred years ago, by evil men for evil ends, was isolated from the Christian world, and torn from the unity of Christ. Since that time, what has been the religious history of England? The schism which rent England from the Divine Tradition of Faith, rent it also from the source of certainty; the division which severed England from the unity of the Church throughout the world planted the principle of schism in England itself. England, carried away from Catholic unity, fell as a landslip from the shore, rending itself by its weight and mass. England, Scotland, Ireland, parted from each other, each with a religion of its own, each with its rule of faith. With schism came contradiction; with contradiction uncertainty, debate, and doubt.

Nor did it stop here. That same principle of

schism which rent asunder these three kingdoms propagated itself still further. In each country division followed division. Each Protestant church, as it was established, contained within itself the principle both of its creation and dissolution, namely, private judgment. And private judgment, working out its result in individual minds, caused schism after schism; until we are told by a writer, Protestant himself, that in the seventeenth century, during the high time of Protestant ascendency, the sects of England amounted to between one and two hundred.

But there are causes and events nearer to our day which render it more than ever necessary to turn back again to the only foundations of certainty, and lay once more the basis of faith The establishment so long by many believed to be a Church, a body with a tradition of three hundred years, upheld by the power of this mighty nation, maintained by the sanction of law and legislature, invested with dignity and titles of state, possessing vast endowments, not of land or gold alone, but of that which is more precious, of treasures which the Catholic Church had gathered, and of which it was rudely spoiled; universities, colleges, and schools: that vast body, cultivated in intellect, embracing the national life in all its strength and ripeness, in an hour of trial was questioned of its faith, and prevaricated in its answer. It was bid to speak as a teacher sent from God; it could not, because God had not sent it. And thus the last remaining hope of certainty among Protestant bodies in this land revealed its own impotence to teach. The body which men fondly believed to partake of the divine office of the Church, proclaimed that alike in its mission and its message it was human.

What then do we see in this land? Sects without number, perpetually subdividing; each equally confident, all contradictory; and that dominant communion which claims to be authoritative in teaching, itself confounded by internal contradictions of its own. How has this come to pass? It is because the Rule of Faith is lost, and the principle of certainty destroyed. Put a familiar illustration: suppose that in this teeming commercial city, where men, in fret and fever from sunrise to sunset, buy and sell, barter and bargain, the rules of calculation and the laws of number were to become extinct; what error would ensue, what litigation, what bankruptcy, and what ruin! Or suppose that in this great mercantile empire, whose fleets cover the seas, the science of astronomy and the art of navigation were to perish; the shores of all the world would be strewn with our wrecks. So it is in the spiritual world. The Rule of Faith once lost, souls wander and perish. The effect of this is that men have come to state, as scientifically certain, that there is no definite doctrine in revelation. As if, indeed, truth had no definite outline. And we find in serious and even good men an enmity against the definite statement of religious truth. They call it dogmatism. The Athanasian Creed they cannot away with. It is too precise and too presumptuous. They feel as men who turn suddenly upon the image of our crucified Lord. They start at it from its very definiteness; and as the sight of a crucifix unexpectedly produces a shock, so will the definite statement of truth. It forces home the reality of faith. People now-a-days assume that religious truth can have no definite outline, and that each man must discover and define it for himself. And however definite he may choose to be, one law is binding equally upon us all. No one must be certain. Each must concede to his neighbor as much certainty as he claims for himself. The objective certainty of truth is gone. The highest rule of certainty to each is the conviction of his own understanding. And this, in the revelation of God; in that knowledge which is life eternal.

I. In answer, then, I say, that all knoweledge must be definite; that without definiteness there is no true knowledge. To tell us that we may have religious knowledge which is not definite, is to tell us that we may have color which is not distinguishable. Every several truth is as distinct as the several colors in the rainbow. Blend them, and you have only confusion. So it is in religious knowledge. Doctrines definite as the stars in heaven, when clouded by the obscurities of the human mind, lose their definiteness, and pass from sight.

Is not this true in every kind of knowledge? Take science, for example. What would a mathematician think of a diagram which is not definite? What would any problem of physical science be, as in optics, or in mechanics, or engineering, or in any of the arts whereby man subjugates nature to his use, if it were not definite? How could it be expressed, by what calculus could it be treated? What, again, is history which is not definite? History which is not the record of definite fact is mythology, fable, and rhapsody. Where history ceases to be definite, it begins to be fabulous. Or take moral science; what are moral laws which are not definite? A law which is not definite carries with it no obligation. If the law cannot be stated, it cannot be known; if not known, it has no claim on our obedience. Unless it definitively tell me what I am to do and what I am not to do, it has no jurisdiction over my conscience. And as in human knowledge, so, above all, in divine. If there be any knowledge which is severely and precisely definite, it is the knowledge which God has revealed of Himself. Finite indeed it is, but definite always: finite as our sight of the earth, the form of which is round; and yet because our narrow sight can compass no more, to us it seems one broad expanse.

Again, take an example from the highest knowledge. When we speak of wisdom, goodness, or power, we carry our mind upward to the attributes of God. When we see these moral qualities reproduced in a finite being, we call them still by the same titles. So with knowledge. What is knowledge in God but an infinite and definite apprehension of uncreated and eternal truth? The knowledge which God has of himself and of His works is a science divine, the example and type of all. To descend from the divine perfection; what is knowledge in the angels but equally definite, though in a finite intelligence? And what was the knowledge of man before the fall, but, though finite, definite still? What, then, is the knowledge which God has restored to man through revelation but a definite knowledge, a participation of His own? The truth which has been revealed, what is it in the mind of God who reveals it, but one, harmonious and distinct? What was that knowledge as revealed by the Holy Spirit on the day of Pentecost, but one, harmonious and distinct? What was the conception of that knowledge in inspired men, but one, harmonious and distinct also? And what was that knowledge when communicated by those who were inspired to those who believed, but one, harmonious and distinct as before? And what is this unity and harmony and distinctness of knowledge, which God revealed of Himself through Jesus Christ, but the faith we confess in our creed? Our baptismal faith, its substance and its letter, the explicit and the implicit meaning, article by article, is as definite, severe, and precise, as any problem in science. It is of the nature of truth to be so; and where definiteness ends, knowledge ceases.

Observe, then, the distinction between finite knowledge and definite knowledge. Is not science definite? Yet it is also finite. The theory of gravitation, definite as it is, is finite too. The theory of electricity is definite as far as we know it, but finite also. Go through the whole range of physical sciences, what is it but an example of the same condition of knowledge, definiteness in conception with finiteness of reach? What has astronomy revealed to us? The starry heavens, in which we trace the laws and revolutions of heavenly bodies. We find centre after centre, and orbit beyond orbit, until at last we reach what has been long fixed upon as the centre of the universe; and yet even here, science now tells us that probably this, our central point, which we believed to be fixed, is again itself a planet revolving around some mightier centre which science cannot attain. Here, then, are the conditions of definiteness and finiteness combined. So in revealed truth. If we have not a definite knowledge of what we believe, we may be sure we have no true knowledge of it.

II. But, further, it is evident that knowledge must also be certain. When we speak of certainty, we mean one of two things. Sometimes we say, that a thing is certain; at other times, that we are certain. When we say *a truth* is certain, we mean, that the proofs of that truth are either self-evident, or so clear as to exclude all doubt. This is certainty on the part of the object proposed to our intelligence. But when we say *we* are certain, we mean that we are inwardly convinced, by the application of our reason to the matter before us, of the sufficiency of the evidence to prove the truth of it. In us, certainty is rather a moral feeling, a complex state of mind. As light manifests itself by its own nature, but sight is the illumination of the eye; so certainty means truth with its evidences illuminating the intelligence, or, in other words, the inteligence possessed by truth with its evidences.

This we call certainty. I ask, then, is there not this twofold certainty in the revelation which God has given? Was not the revelation which God gave of Himself through Jesus Christ made certain on His part by direct evidence of the Divine act which revealed it? Is it not also certain on our part by the apprehension and faith of the Church? Was not God manifest in the flesh that He might reveal Himself? Did not God dwell on earth that He might teach His truth? Has not God spoken to man that man might know Him? Did not God work miracles that man might believe that He was present? What evidence on the part of God was wanting that men might know that Jesus Christ was indeed the Son of God?

And if there was certainty on the part of God who revealed, was there not certainty also on the part of those that heard? Look back into the sacred history. Had not Prophets and Seers certainty of that which they beheld and heard? Had not Abraham certainty when he saw a dark mist and a smoking furnace, and a fiery lamp moved between the portions of the sacrifice? Was not Moses certain when he beheld the pattern shewn to him on the Mount? Was not Daniel certain when the angel Gabriel flew swiftly and touched him at the time of the evening sacrifice? Were not Apostles and Evangelists certain when they companied with our Lord, and said, "That which was from the beginning, which we have heard, which we have seen with our eyes, which we have diligently looked upon, and our hands have handled, concerning the Word of Life?" Were not the

Twelve certain in the upper chamber? Were they not certain on the day of Pentecost? Was not Paul certain in Arabia, when he learned the Gospel, not of man, nor of flesh and blood, but "by the revelation of Jesus Christ?" Was not John certain in Patmos, when heaven was opened, and the vision of the future was traced before his eye? And were not they certain to whom Patriarchs, Prophets, Seers, Apostles, Evangelists, preached and wrote? Has not the Church of God been certain from that hour to this of the revelation given and received at the first?

What, then, is the first condition of faith but certainty? He that has not certain faith has no faith. We are told that to crave for certainty implies a morbid disposition. Did not Abraham, and Moses, and Daniel, the Apostles and Evangelists desire certainty in faith, and crave to know beyond doubt that God spake to them, and to know with definite clearness what God said? Was this a morbid craving? Surely this is not to be reproved. But rather the contrary disposition is worthy of rebuke. How can we venture to content ourselves with uncertainty in matters where the truth and honor of God and the salvation of our own souls are at stake? This truly is not without sin.

We are told, indeed, that to be certain is inconsistent with faith, that probability is the atmosphere in which faith lives, and that if you extinguish probabilities, faith dies. Did the Apostles then believe the doctrine of the ever-blessed Trinity upon a probability? Did they believe the doctrine of the Incarnation upon conjecture? Was it because they walked in twilight that their faith in their Divine Lord was acceptable?

To what are we come? In this Christian land, once full of light, once in unity with the Church of God, once replenished with truth,—to what are we come? A new virtue is promulgated; to be uncertain of the truth and of the will of God; to hold our faith on probabilities. And yet, what is the very idea of Revelation but a Divine assurance of Truth? Where faith begins uncertainty ends. Because faith terminates upon the veracity of God; and what God has spoken and authenticated to us by Divine authority cannot be uncertain.

I am aware, brethren, that much of what I have said has no application to you. You are the heirs of a Divine inheritance. As the science of astronomy, in its severity and truth, has descended by intellectual tradition from the first simple observations made on the plains of Chaldea down to the abstract and complex demonstrations of these later times, so has the tradition of faith, the science of God, come down to you. You have been born within its sphere. You know it by a manifold assurance, by the certainty of God revealing it, the Scriptures of God recording it, the Church of God preserving it, the Councils of the Church defining it, the Holy See from age to age condemning error and setting its seal upon the faith. You have it brought down to you with imperishable certainty. Your guide is not human but Divine. Why then do I speak to you? Because you have a mission to fulfil. You have to bring others to a share of the same inheritance. I bespeak your charity and your patience in their behalf. I cannot better put before you the state of those who have lost what to you has been preserved, than by a parallel. Suppose I were to write an inscription, and shew it to you. Having read it, the meaning of that inscription passes, so to speak, into the very substance of your mind. It is ineffaceably impressed upon your memory. Then tear it into twenty pieces, and give one piece to twenty men respectively; set them to discover the whole. I know it, because I wrote it; you know it, because you have seen and read it. They know it only in part. They have each a fragment; but they cannot conjecture the rest. So is it with the sects that are around the Church of God. The one inscription, written, not by man, but by the Spirit of God upon the illuminated reason of the Church, has descended perfect and entire until now. But each several sect as it departed from unity carried away a fragment. The children of schismatics inherit a fragment only. As "faith cometh by hearing," so theology cometh by hearing, and the doctrine of the Catholic Church in its harmony, unity, and distinctness, comes by hearing. They who never heard that faith, to whom the science in its fulness has not descended, have but a fragment, from which they labor in vain to conjecture the remainder. You can help them. Not by controversy; not by destroying what they have already. To destroy even a fragment of the Truth is Satan's controversy. The divine way of establishing faith among men is not to throw down, but to build up: to add, to develop, to perfect. Every truth that a man possesses is so far a pledge that you have a share in him, that so far he is with you. Hold him fast by that truth. Add to it the next which follows in Divine order; and so in patience and in charity lead him on from truth to truth, as by the links of a chain, and bind him to the altar of God.

And now, of those who reject the principles I have stated, and deny to theology the character of definiteness and certainty, I would ask two questions:—

1. First, I would ask, What do you believe? Put it in words. Conceive it in thought. Fix your mind's eye upon it. Put it in writing in some

silent hour: know at least what it is. As you value your eternal soul, as you believe that the end of your being is to be united with God eternally, and that the means to that eternal union is the knowledge of God in Christ Jesus, be not content a day to abide in uncertainty and indefiniteness concerning the truth, which you know to be vitally necessary to your salvation.

Again, I say put it in words. First, what do you believe of the Godhead? You believe in the Father, Son, and Holy Ghost? This you hold definitely and without a doubt. What do you believe of the Incarnation of the Son of God? That in Him two whole and perfect natures are united in one person, never to be divided. You believe the Godhead, presence, and office of the Holy Ghost? But there remain other articles of your creed. We come next to "the Holy Catholic Church." What do you believe in this article of Faith? Will you say, "We have definite and certain knowledge of the former articles, but not of the latter. When I come to 'the Holy Catholic Church' I come to a region where uncertainty is lawful?" But uncertainty is doubt, and doubt and faith are contradictory. You may not doubt in your baptismal faith, or be uncertain as to the articles of your creed. May we make an open question, for example, of the resurrection of the dead? Why not be also uncertain whether or no the Holy Spirit of God be in the world now; or, being now in the world, whether He have a present office to teach? You believe this; but why believe this, and doubt of other doctrines of the same creed? And if you believe that the Holy Spirit does still teach the world, how does He teach? Each several man by immediate inspiration? If not, then how? You will say perhaps, that He teaches through the Church. But if through the Church, through what Church? How are we the better or the wiser by knowing that the Spirit of God teaches the world at this hour, and that He has an organ through which to speak, if we know not which, nor where that organ is? How then shall you know that you hear His voice? If you knew that of twelve men who stood before you, one only possessed a secret upon which your life depended, would you be careless to know which man bore the treasure in his possession? Why then may you be indifferent to ascertain which is the accredited messenger upon whom your faith depends?

Try therefore to define your meaning. You say you believe a Church, because your baptismal faith says, "I believe one Holy Catholic Church:" holy, because the Holy Spirit teaches in it; Catholic, because throughout all the world; and one. Why *one?* Why do you say that you believe in *one* God? Because there is not more than one God. Why *one*

Lord? Because not two. Why *one* baptism? Because one alone. Why *one* faith? Because no other. All these are numerically *one*. Why then *one* Church? Because numerically one; two there cannot be. Through that one Church speaks the one Spirit of the one God, teaching the one faith in which is salvation. Which then is this true and only Teacher sent from God? You look about you, and see a Church in Greece, in Russia, in America, in England, and in Rome. Which of all these is the one only true? Can you be content with this guess-work instead of faith?

2. And further: I would ask another question. I have asked you what you believe; I will now ask you *why* you believe it; upon what basis of certainty you are convinced of it, and why? Do you say that you have applied the best powers of your understanding to it? So have others who contradict you. Why are you more surely right than they are? You have not had a message from heaven, sent by special indulgence to make you sure, while others wander. What then is the basis of your certainty? The persuasion of your own mind is not enough. At that rate all men are certain. False coins pass in every land; false miracles take the semblance of true. The whole world is full of counterfeits. What I ask you is this: How do you distinguish between your certainty and the certainty of other

men, so as to know that their certainty is human, and yours divine? Why are they wrong, and you right? Where is the test to determine this? You know it cannot exist within you, for every body may claim the same. You look then without you and around to find it.

Well, you will perhaps tell us that you have inherited the faith you hold. The inheritance of faith, that is a divine principle. We bow before the principle of inheritance. But why did you cut off the entail of your forefathers? Why, three hundred years ago, did you cut off the entail of that inheritance? If it be not cut off, why is the contest? If it be cut off, why was it cut off? To inherit the faith is the divine rule. It needs only one thing, infallibility, to secure it. It needs only one support to give it substance and certainty; a divine tradition flowing from the Throne of God through Prophets, Seers, Apostles, Evangelists, Martyrs, Saints, and Doctors in one world-wide stream, ever deepening, never changing, from the beginning until now. Shew this divine certainty as the basis of your conviction, and then inherit both truth and faith. But the inheritance of opinion in a family, or a diocess, or a province, or a nation, what is it? Human in the beginning, and human to the end: "the traditions of men."

You say you have inherited the faith, and that

this is the Church of your forefathers. Go back three hundred years ago, and ask those priests of God who stood then at the altar how they would expound the faith you still profess to hold. Ask them what they believed while they ministered in cope and chasuble. Go back to the Apostle of England who first bore hither again the light of the Gospel after Saxon paganism had darkened this fair land. Ask St. Augustin what he believed of those words, "Thou art Peter, and upon this rock I will build My Church." Give your exposition, and ask his. What would he have taught you of visible unity? What would he teach you of the Church of God? Ask him, Is it one numerically, or one only by metaphor? Is it visible, that all men may see "the City seated on a mountain," or invisible, that men may weary themselves, and never find it? Has it a head on earth, representing its Divine Head in heaven? Or has it no head, and may it set up many of its own? What would he have taught you of your baptismal creed? Or that great saint who sent him from the Apostolic throne, what would he have testified to you of those doctrines of faith which you are taught to look upon as errors? Ask Gregory, first and greatest of the name, what he believed of the powers left by the Incarnate Son to His Church on earth: what he taught of the power of the keys transmitted by his predecessors in lineal descent from the hands of his Divine Lord? Ask what he taught of the power of absolution in the sacrament of penance; what he believed of the Reality on the altar, and of the Holy Sacrifice daily offered in all the world; of the Communion of Saints ever interceding, by us ever invoked; of the intermediate state of departed souls, purifying for the kingdom of God. Ask Gregory, saint and doctor, to whom we owe the faith, what he taught of those doctrines which you have rejected.

If the disciple and his master, if he that was sent, and he that sent him, were to come now and tread the shore of this ancient river, whither would they turn to worship? Would they go to the stately minister, raised by their sons in the faith, where even now rests a sainted king of Catholic England? Would they bend their steps thither to worship the God of their fathers, and their Incarnate Lord from whom their mission and their faith descended? Or would they not rather go to some obscure altar in its neighborhood, where an unknown despised priest daily offers the Holy Sacrifice in communion with the world-wide Church of God?

If, then, you claim inheritance as the foundation of your faith, be true to your principle, and it will load you home. Trifle not with it. Truth bears the stamp of God, and truth changes man to the likeness of God. Trifle not with the pleadings of the Holy Spirit within you; for He has a delicate touch, and sensitively shrinks from wilfulness and unbelief. If truth struggle within you, follow it faithfully. Tread close upon the light that you possess. Count all things loss that you may win truth, without which the inheritance of God's kingdom is not ours. Labor for it, and weary yourselves until you find it. And forgot not that if your religion be indefinite, you have no true knowledge of your Saviour; and if your belief be uncertain, it is not the faith by which we can be saved.

LECTURE II.

THE CHURCH A HISTORICAL WITNESS.

St. John xvii. 3.

"This is life everlasting, that they may know Thee, the only true God, and Jesus Christ whom Thou hast sent."

Before we go on to the subject that stands next in order, it will be well to re-state the conclusions at which we have thus far arrived.

From these words of our Divine Lord, we have seen that the end of man is eternal life, and the means to that end the knowledge of God in Jesus Christ. Union with God in knowledge, love, and worship, is life eternal. And that man might attain to this end of his creation, God has revealed Himself to us in His Son. We have, therefore, noted the error of those who say that in Revelation doctrine is either not definite, or not certain. It is manifest that all knowledge must be definite; for if it be not definite, we may have guess, or conjecture, or probability, but true knowledge we cannot have. We have seen also that it must be certain; and that unless we have certainty we can have no faith, because the mind cannot rest upon uncertainty, as hunger cannot sate itself on air.

We have obtained, then, two principles; the one, that knowledge, though indeed it be finite, as it must be in a finite intelligence, is nevertheless, so far as it is known to us, perfectly definite. It is as a complex mathematical figure which we see only in part, but in all we can see is perfect, harmonious, and proportionate, capable of being understood, calculated, and expressed. Being in the mind of God one, harmonious and distinct, it is cast on the limited sphere of man's intelligence in its unity, harmony, and distinctness. The other principle is, that the knowledge which God has given us of Himself is, in every sense, certain. We cannot conceive that the contradictory of that which God has spoken can be true, or that Prophets and Apostles were uncertain of what they believed and taught.

And now we will go on to examine what is the foundation upon which this certainty descends to us. It is, in one word, the authority of the Church of God. But this authority of the Church is twofold: it is either the outward and extrinsic, which I may call the human and historical authority; or it is the inward and intrinsic, that is, the supernatural and the divine authority. The latter we must consider hereafter. For the present we will examine only the outward or historical authority of the Church, upon which the certainty of revelation as a fact in history is known to us.

All who have traced the history of the faith know that there is no doctrine which has not been made the subject of controversy. Look at the records of Christianity, and you will find that heresy began with the first publication of the truth. In the first age, we find heresies assailing the doctrine of the Godhead of the Father, the Creator of the world. In the next age heresies assailed the doctrine of the Godhead of the Son; later again, the doctrine of the Godhead of the Holy Ghost; next the doctrine of holy Sacraments; later still, the doctrine of the Church itself. A vast schism arose, justifying itself by denying the existence and the authority of the visible Church as such. And because the existence and authority of the visible Church was so denied, the foundation of certainty was broken up, and the principle of uncertainty introduced. Age by age, and article by article, the faith has been denied, until we come down to a period when the characteristic heresy of the day is, not a denial of the Godhead of the Father, or of the Son, or of the Holy Ghost, and the like, though these too are denied, but the denial of the foundation of certainty in faith. The master-heresy of this day, the fountain and source of all heresy, is this, that men have come first to deny, and then to disbelieve the existence in the world of a foundation, divinely laid, upon which revealed truth can certainly rest.

Let us ask those who deny the existence of this basis of certainty, upon what do they rest when they believe in the fact of a revelation? The revelation was not made to them personally. It was not made to-day. It was made to others: it was made eighteen hundred years ago. By what means, I ask, are men now certain that eighteen hundred years ago, to other men, in other lands, a revelation from God was given? They are forced back upon history. They were not there to see or hear. Revelation does not spring up by inspiration in their inward consciousness. They are, therefore, thrown upon history; they are compelled to go to the testimony of others. All men who at this hour believe in the Advent of the Son of God, and in the fact of the day of Pentecost, all alike rest upon history. Not but that Catholics rest on more (of this, however, hereafter); but they who do not rest upon the divine office of the Church rest on history alone. Then, I ask, by what criterion are they certain that their historical views are true? Let them throw the rule of their examination into some form of words. Unless they can put into intelligible words the principle of certainty upon which they rest, it is either useless or false: useless, if it cannot be stated, for if it cannot be stated, it cannot be applied; false, if the nature of it be such that it will not admit of expression.

I would beseech any who are resting upon such a certainty as this, not to confound a sensation of positiveness with the sense of certainty. The sense of certainty is a Divine gift. It is the inward testimony of our whole intelligent nature. A sensation of positiveness springs out of obstinacy, or prejudice. Let them not confound the resolution to believe themselves in the right with the reason for knowing that they are in the truth. Let them analyse deeper, and find what is their principle, and state that principle in intelligible words. To take an example. We all believe, apart from revelation, that the world was created. How so? We proceed to prove it. The world is not eternal, for then it would be God. It did not make itself, for that is a contradiction. Therefore, it remains of necessity that it had a maker. I ask them only to be as definite as this: for life is short and eternity is long, and we are saved by truth; and truth which is not definite is no truth to us; and indefinite statements have no certainty; and without certainty there is no faith.

In answer to this we are told that all men can

read the Holy Scriptures, and that this is enough. I reply, Scripture is not Scripture except in the right sense of Scripture. Your will after you are dead is not your testament unless it be interpreted according to your intention. The words and syllables of your testament may be so interpreted as to contradict your purpose. The will of the deceased is the intention of the deceased known by his testament. So of Holy Scripture. Holy Scripture is Holy Scripture only in the right sense of Holy Scripture.

But we are further told, that notwithstanding these superficial contradictions, all good men agree in essentials. First, then, I ask, What are essentials? Who has the power to determine what is essential and what is not? By whose judgment are we to ascertain it? The Church knows only one essential truth, and that is, the whole revelation of God. It knows of no power to determine between truth and truth, and to say, "though God has revealed this, we need not believe it." The whole revelation of God comes to us with its intrinsic obligation on our faith, and we receive it altogether as God's word. They who speak of all good men agreeing in essentials, mean this: "I believe what I think essential, and I give my neighbor leave to believe what he thinks essential." Their agreement is only this, not to molest each other: but they mutilate the revelation of God.

In opposition to these opinions, let us state the grounds of our own certainty.

I. We believe, then, that we have no knowledge of the way of salvation through grace, except from the revelation of God. No one can deny this. It is a truism that we have no knowledge of the way of redemption by grace except through divine revelation. The whole world is witness of the fact. For four thousand years the world wandered on, and knew not the way of grace except by a thread of light which from Adam to Enoch, and from Enoch to Noe, and from Noe to Abraham, and from Abraham to Moses, and from Moses to the promised Seed, ran down, keeping alive in the world the expectation of a Redeemer. Outside this path of light the way of grace was not known; nor was it known even there except by revelation.

And round about that solitary light, what was there? Was there a knowledge of the way of salvation through grace? The heathen nations, their polytheism, their idolatry, their morality, their literature, their public and their private life, do these give testimony to the way of grace? Take their schools, their philosophies, their greatest intellects, what do they prove? One of the greatest practical intellects of the Eastern world believed that matter was eternal, and that the soul of the world was God. The loftiest of all in speculation was blind when he came to treat of the first laws of purity. In the west, the greatest orators, poets, and philosophers, either believed in no God at all, or in a blind and imaginary deity, stripped of personality. This was all that Nature could do. Nature without revelation had no true knowledge of God, and absolutely none of salvation through grace.

It was not until four thousand years had passed that the way of salvation through grace was revealed. Look at the mightiest effort Nature in its own strength ever made,—the empire of Rome; that vast power extending itself in all the world; the whole earth wondering at the onward march of its victorious armies; races falling back before its legions; its frontiers expanding whithersoever they trod; a mighty, world-wide dominion, whose capital spread from the Mediterranean to the Alban hills, in circuit sixty or seventy miles, within which nations dwelt together: the palace of the aristocracy of the earth; for magnificence, splendor, and civilization, never exceeded among mankind. Human nature here was taxed to its utmost strength: human intelligence reached its utmost bound; and what knew Rome of the way of grace, or of salvation through Jesus Christ? What was the morality of Rome? What was its religion? It was the high place of all the gods; the deities of the greater and lesser nations, and of the surrounding cities which it conquered, were incorporated with its own superstitions. All impieties were in veneration, and every falsehood had its shrine. Only truth was persecuted, only one worship was forbidden; and that, the only doctrine and the only worship not of this world. Nature did its utmost; the intelligence of man bore testimony to all it could attain. The Babel of confusion was built to teach mankind for ever that human nature without God could never rise to a knowledge of the way of grace.

The manifestation of God in the flesh; the effusion of light and revelation through the Holy Spirit; the setting up of the mystical ladder at the head of which the Lord stands, and on which Angels ascend and descend; the gathering together of truths that had wandered to and fro on earth; and the uniting of all in one hierarchy of faith: nothing less was needed before man could know the way of eternal life.

It is certain, then, that we have no natural knowledge of the way of salvation through grace; that is, through the Incarnation, the Atonement, the mystical Body of Christ; through the Sacraments, which are the channels of the Holy Spirit. Without revelation we have no true knowledge of sin, whereby we forfeited our sonship; nor of regeneration, whereby we regain it; nor of the relation of grace to the free-will of man; and the like. But all these are doctrines upon which union with God and eternal life depend, and yet of these not a whisper was heard on earth until revelation came by Jesus Christ.

II. But, further, we believe, in the second place, that as we have no knowledge of the way of salvation through grace, except from the revelation of God, so neither have we any certainty what that revelation was, except through the Church of God As the fountain is absolutely one and no other, so the channel through which it flows is absolutely one and no other. As there is no source of certainty but revelation, so there is no channel through which it can flow but the Church of God. For certainty as to the revelation given eighteen hundred years ago, of the Church we needs must learn. To what other can we go? Who besides has the words of eternal life? Shall we go to the nations of the world? Can they teach the faith which they knew not before Christ came, neither have since believed? Shall we go to the fragments of Christendom broken off from age to age by heresy and schism? Their testimony is but local, limited, and contradictory. What certainty can the Monophysite, Eutychian, Nestorian, or Protestant, give of the day of Pentecost? To whom, then, shall we go? To that one mystical body which came down from the upper chamber to possess the earth; to that one moral person upon whom the Holy Spirit then descended; to that kingdom of the God of heaven, which, spreading from Jerusalem throughout all lands, penetrated into every country, province, and city, erecting its thrones, ascending in might and power, expanding throughout the earth, gathering together its circumference, filling up the area of its circuit, until the world became Christian; and then sat in sovereignty, displacing and replacing the empire of the world. This universal kingdom, one and indivisible, reigning continuous and perpetual in unbroken succession from the day of Pentecost, was the eye-witness and the ear-witness of revelation. This one moral person alone can say, "When the Word made flesh spake, I heard; when the tongues of fire descended from heaven, I saw: with my senses I perceived the presence of God; with my intelligence I understood His voice; with my memory I retain to this hour the knowledge of what I then heard and saw; with my changeless conciousness I testify what was spoken." To this one, and this one only witness in the world, can we go for certainty.

Put the case thus. Will you go to the Monophysite, Eutychian, or Nestorian heresies, ancient as they are, which separated from the Church of Christ in the fifth and sixth centuries? Will they bear witness? Yes; but only a partial testimony. They were witnesses so long as they were united to the one Church; but their testimony ceased when they separated from it. They are witnesses so far as they agree with that one Church, but not when they contradict it. The testimony derived from separated bodies amounts to this: it is the borrowed light which even in separation they receive from the Church itself.

And as with early, so with later heresies. Shall we go to the separated Greek communion, which claims to be the only orthodox Church? Will that give a trustworthy testimony? Yes; so far as it agrees with the body from which it departed. Its witness after the separation is but local. Shall we go to the great division of these later times, to the huge crumbling Protestantism of the last three centuries? Is there in it any sect descending from the day of Pentecost? When did it begin? A hundred years ago, probably, or it may be two, or at most three hundred years ago. At that time a traceable change produced it. Does Protestantism reach upward to the original revelation? Has it a succession of sense, reason, memory, and consciousness, uniting it with the day of Pentecost?

If, then, what has been said as to the only source and channel of knowledge and certainty be true, sufficient reason has been shewn to make every one who is resting on the testimony of bodies separated from the universal Church mistrust his confidence. Must he not say, "Eighteen hundred years ago a revelation was given; my life reaches but a span, my memory but a few years; how do I know what passed on that day? How shall they tell me whose life, like my own, touches only upon the last generation? I go to this and to that separated communion, but they all fall short. There is one and one only living witness in the world, which, as it touches on the present hour in which I live, unites me by a lineal consciousness, by a living intelligence, with the moment when, in the third hour of the day, 'there came a sound from heaven as of a mighty wind coming, and filled the whole house.'"

Let it be remembered that I am speaking of the external authority of the Church simply as an historical argument. We will confine ourselves for the present to this alone. I put it forward as it was cited by a philosophical historian, one of the greatest of this age, who, having passed through the windings of German unbelief, found at last his rest in the one True Fold. Explaining the ground of his submission, Schlegel gave this reason; that he found the testimony of the Catholic Church to be the greatest historical authority on earth for the events of the past. It is in this sense I am speaking.

And therefore, when I use the word *authority*, I mean evidence. The word "authority" may be used in two senses. It may either signify power, such as the jurisdiction which the Church has over the souls committed to its trust; or it may mean evidence, as when we say, we have a statement on the authority, or evidence, of an eye-witness.

Suppose, then, we were to reject this highest historical evidence; suppose we were to say that the authority of the Catholic Church, though of great weight, is not conclusive: I would ask, what historical evidence remains beyond it? To whom else shall we go? Is there any other authority upon which we can rest? If we receive not the authority of the Universal Church, we must descend from higher to lower ground, we must come down to the partial authority of a local church. Will this be to ascend in the scale of certainty? If the testimony of the Universal Church be not the *maximum* of historical evidence in the world, where shall we find it? Shall we find it in the church of Greece, or of America, or of England? Shall we find it in the church of a province, or in the church of a diocess? If the Universal Episcopate be not the maximum of external evidence, where shall it be found? And, in fact, they who reject the evidence of the Universal Church for the primitive faith, necessarily rest their belief on the authority of a local body, or on the authority of a man. It was by divine intuition that our Lord said, "Call none your father upon earth;

for they who will not believe the Church of God must be in bondage to human teachers. If they are Calvinists, they must be in bondage to Calvin; or Lutherans, to Luther; or Arians, to Arius; or if they be members of a church separated from Catholic unity, they must be in bondage to its self-constituted head. The ultimate authority in which they trust is human. From this false confidence in man the Catholic Church alone can redeem us. We trust not in the judgment of an individual, howsoever holy or wise, but in the witness of an universal and perpetual body, to which teachers and taught alike are subject; and because all are in subjection to the Church, all are redeemed from bondage to individual teachers and the authority of men.

Thus far we have spoken of the Church as a mere human witness. To us, indeed, brethren, its voice is not mere human testimony. God has provided for faith a certainty which cannot fail; the mystical Body of Christ, changeless and indestructible, spread throughout the world. Wonderful creation of God; but far more wonderful if it be the creation of man: if, after all man's failures to construct an imperishable kingdom, to hold together the human intelligence in one conviction, the human will in one discipline, and the human heart in one bond of love; if, after four thousand years of failure, mere human power framed the Catholic Church, endowed it with resistless power of expansion, and quickened it with the life of universal charity. More wonderful far, if it was man's work to create the great science of theology, in which the baptismal formula, "I baptise thee in the name of the Father, and of the Son, and of the Holy Ghost," expands into the creed, and the creed again expands into the science of God on which the illuminated reason of eighteen hundred years has spent itself. Wonderful, indeed, if this be a mere human creation! To us it is the work and voice of God; to us the line of Bishops and of Councils by which the Faith has been declared in perpetual succession is the testimony which God Himself has countersigned, the witness God Himself has sent. This continuous testimony from the Council of Arles to the Council of Nice, from the Council of Nice to that of Chalcedon, from Chalcedon to Lateran, from Lateran to Lyons, and from Lyons to Trent, is one harmonious science, ever expanding as a reflection of the mind of God; preserving and unfolding before us the one Truth revealed in the beginning, in its unity and harmony and distinctness. This is the basis of our certainty.

What is the history of the Catholic Church but the history of the intellect of Christendom? What do we see but two lines, the line of faith and the line of heresy, running side by side in every age;

and the Church, as a living Judge, sitting sovereign and alone with unerring discernment, dividing truth from error with a sharp two-edged sword? Every several altar, and every several See, gives testimony to the same doctrines; and all conspiring voices ascend into the testimony of that One See, which in its jurisdiction is universal, and in its presence every where; that one See, the foundation-stones of which were cemented in the blood of thirty Pontiffs; that See which recorded its archives in the vaults of catacombs, and when the world was weary with persecuting, ascended to possess itself of imperial basilicas. This is the witness upon whose testimony we securely rest. The Church is a living history of the past. Cancel this, and what record is there left? If Rome be gone, where is Christendom?

LECTURE III.

THE CHURCH A DIVINE WITNESS.

Sᴛ. Jᴏʜɴ xvii. 3.

"*This is life everlasting, that they may know Thee, the only true God, and Jesus Christ whom Thou hast sent.*"

Tʜᴇ truths which we have already affirmed are these: that the end of man is eternal life through the knowledge of God revealed in Jesus Christ; that this knowledge of God, being a participation of the Divine knowledge, is definite and certain; and that as there is but one fountain of this Divine knowledge in Revelation, so there is but one channel of this Divine certainty in the Church. We have seen also that the authority of the Church of God on earth is the highest, or maximum of evidence, even in a human and historical sense, of the past; that unless we rest upon this evidence, we must descend in the scale of certainty.

But we have as yet considered the Church only in

its external, human, and historical character: there still remains for us a deeper and diviner truth. I have spoken of the authority of the Church only as history of the past; but, be it ever remembered, that between the Protestant and the Catholic there is this difference. To the Protestant, history must be a record of the past gathered from documents by criticism, fallible as the judge who applies it. To the Catholic, history, though it be of the past, is of the present also. The Church is a living history of the past. It is the page of history still existing, open before his eyes. Antiquity to the Catholic is not a thing gone by; it is here, still present. As childhood and youth are summed up by manhood in our personal identity, so is antiquity ever present in the living Church. If Christianity, then, be historical, Catholicism is Christianity.

Let us therefore proceed to the deeper and diviner, that is, to the interior and intrinsic authority of the Church of Christ. We believe, then, that the interior and intrinsic authority of the Church is the presence of the Holy Spirit; that the ultimate authority upon which we believe is no less than the perpetual presence of our Lord Jesus Christ teaching always by His Spirit in the world.

I. And, first, let us ascertain what points of agreement exist between us and those who are in separation from us. We are all agreed that the only subject-matter of faith is the original revelation of God. They who most oppose us profess to be jealous above all men to restrain all doctrine to the bounds of the original revelation.

We agree, then, at the outset, that the subject-matter of our faith is, and can only be, the original revelation of God. To that revelation nothing may be added; from it nothing may be taken away. As God in the beginning created the sun in the heavens with its perfect disc, and no skill or power of man can make its circumference greater or less, so Divine revelation is a work of God's omnipotence, and no man can add to it, or take from it. In this also we are agreed. But there are other principles no less vital than these. Let those who are so jealous for this law of truth remember, that as we may neither take from nor add to revelation, so neither may we misinterpret or pervert it; neither fix upon it our private meaning, nor make it speak our sense. We must receive it as God gave it, in its perfect fulness; with its true sense and purport as it was revealed.

It were good, then, if they who are so jealous of supposed additions to the faith, were equally jealous of evident and manifest perversions of the same. It would be well if those who are so hostile to interpretations of Holy Scripture made by the Catholic Church, were equally hostile to interpretations made by every man severally of that same book. Let us proceed more exactly; and as we agree that nothing may be added to or taken from that revelation, so let us jealously demand that nothing in it shall be misinterpreted, nor its sense wrested aside, nor its meaning perverted.

But here begin our differences. How are we to attain the right sense of Holy Scripture? It is a divine book, and contains the mind of God. How, then, shall we know what is His mind? By what rule or test shall we know with certainty that we have attained the meaning which the Divine Spirit intended in that revelation? We have here many tests and many rules offered to us. Some tell us that Scripture is so self-evident that the man who reads it must understand. If that be so, why do they that read it contradict each other? Facts refute the theory. If Holy Scripture be so clear, why are there so many contradictory interpretations?

But is it so clear? When the English reader has before him for the New Testament the Greek text, and for the Old Testament the Hebrew text —neither of which languages he reads—where is the self-evidence of his text then? How does he know that the book before him truly represents the original? How can he prove it? How can he establish the identity between the original and the translation? How can he tell that the book before him is authentic or genuine, or that the text is pure? For all this he depends on others.

But let us take this argument as it is stated. Is Scripture, then, so self-evident that no one who reads it can mistake its sense? If it be self-evident to the individual, it is self-evident to the Church. If the text is so clear to every man who reads it, then it has been clear to every Saint of God from the beginning. If this book is so plain that men cannot mistake it, then the Pastors and Teachers of the Church have handed down its clear and certain interpretation. Why are individuals so sharp-sighted and unerring, and the Saints of God at all times blind? This is but the recoil of their own argument. Let Holy Scripture be as clear and self-evident as they say, then I claim in virtue of that clearness that the Saints of God in all ages have rightly understood its sense.

II. But let us pass onward. We see that they who claim to interpret this book, with all its clearness, contradict each other, and that their rule fails in their own hand. Therefore, the wiser among Protestants say, that to the text of Scripture must be added right reason to interpret it. Right reason, no doubt: but whose reason is right reason? Every man's reason is to himself right reason. The reason of Calvin was right reason to Calvin, and the reason of Luther to Luther; but the misfortune is, that what is right reason to one man is not so to another man. What then is this right reason? It means a certain inward intellectual discernment which each man claims for himself. But how did he become possessed of it? Whence did he receive this endowment? And if he has it, have not others the same? This right reason which men claim whereby to interpret Scripture for themselves must be one of two things: either the individual or the collective reason; that is, the reason of each man for himself, or the accumulated reason of Christians taken together. But will any man say that his reason is to him so certain and unerring a rule that he is able to take the page of Scripture, and by the powers of his understanding infallibly interpret it? For such a claim as this a man must have either a particular inspiration, which considerate men dare not profess, or he must substitute a sensation of positiveness for a sense of certainty.

If, then, this right reason comes to nothing in the individual, does it mean the collective reason of the many? If so, it falls back into a principle valid and certain. What is the collective reason of Christians but the tradition of Christendom? The intellectual agreement of the Saints of God, what is it but the illuminated reason of those that believe? Here we touch upon a great principle; let us follow its guidance.

After the division which rent England from the unity of the Church, and therefore from the certainty of faith; when men began to re-examine the foundations which Protestantism had uprooted, there arose in the Anglican Church a school of writers, acute and sincere enough both to see and to confess that the principle of private judgment is the principle of unbelief. They began to reconstruct a foundation for their faith, and were compelled to return once more to the old basis of Catholic theology. We can trace from about the middle of the reign of Elizabeth down to the great revolution of 1688, a theological school which sprung up within the Established Church, basing itself upon Catholic tradition, and claiming to found its faith not upon private judgment, but upon the rule of St. Vincent of Lerins, namely, on that which was believed "at all times, everywhere, and by all men." This school, for it never indeed was more, has in it names honored and loved, names ever dear to those who have been partakers with them. They were no common men; their lives were ascetic, their intellects capacious, and their erudition deep. They inherited a position which they would never have chosen; a position in many respects vague, and for which time had not yet supplied a practical comment; and they endeavored to defend by learning that which had owed its origin to violence; their position created their theory. They suffered for their opinions, and passed through trying times with great integrity. Had they not had these virtues, they would not have been so long received as authority. They kept alive an illusion that the Anglican church was indeed a portion still of the great Catholic empire which rests upon the unity and infallibility of the Church of God; an illusion indeed, but not without its providential use. For look at the countries where such a belief has been extinct from the beginning; at the Socinianism of Switzerland, the Protestantism of France, the Rationalism of Germany; and say whither England might have gone down if this illusion had not been permitted to exist? They, while they knew it not, did a work for England: a counterwork against the license of Protestant reformation. They were the leaders of a reaction, the fruit of which will be seen hereafter. They laid again in part the foundations of belief; they demonstrated that private judgment is no adequate rule for the interpretation of the faith. They cast men back again upon authority: and put once more into their hands a test. And what is that test, but the historical tradition of the Church, namely, that whatsoever was revealed in the beginning, and believed every where by all men and at all times, is, beyond a doubt, the faith of Pentecost?

But here we touch upon another difficulty even

more pressing and more vital. We have now the test by which to discover the truth; but where is the mind by which that test shall be applied? If the individual reason be not enough in its own powers of discernment to interpret the books of Evangelists and Apostles, one small volume written with the perspicuity of inspiration—if the individual reason be not enough for this, is it able to take the literature of eighteen, or even of the first six centuries, volumes written in many tongues and in all Christian lands, to make survey and analysis of them, to gather together and to pronounce what has been believed by all men, and every where, and at all times? Even in ordinary things, if the question were, What are those universal principles of the common law of England which have been held every where, at all times, and by all common-law judges, would any individual in ordinary life think himself a competent critic? Would he not go to Westminster? Or if the question were, What is the pronunciation or idiom of a language? would he go to books and not to natives? Or, if the question related to the grounds of scientific conclusions, would he buy and pore over treatises of science, instead of asking those whose lives have been devoted to science? Even in music, there are melodies, the accentuation and time of which cannot be written; they can be transmitted only from the voice to the ear. So is it with the transmission of the faith. Though in subjects where the Church has not spoken, individuals may investigate, yet the application of the rule of St. Vincent needs more than the discernment of an individual mind. It needs a judge whose comprehensive survey penetrates the whole matter upon which it judges. And where is the individual that can compass the whole experience of Christendom? Nay, more; it needs a judge who can not only discern for one age, but for the next, and the age succeeding. What benefit is there in a judge that judges in his day, and dies? A perpetual doctrine tested by a perpetual rule needs a perpetual judge. Who judged in the times following the Apostles but the Church in their next successors? Who in the century after, when heresy arose, but the Church in Councils? Who in the heresy of Arius, the heresy of Eutyches, the schism of the Greek Church? Who judged in the middle ages? who in later times? who judges to-day? The same judge always sitting; the same one living body which by the illumination of Pentecost received the Truth. Is it not plain that as every age needs the truth for its redemption, and as our Divine Lord has made provision that every age through the truth shall be redeemed, so at no time from the beginning until now has the world ever been, and at no time from now until the end, shall the world ever be, without a teacher and a judge to declare with final certainty what is the tradition of the faith?

Here then we find ourselves in the presence of the Church. As the subject-matter demands a test, so the test demands a judge. What other judge is there? What other can there be, but that one moral person, continuous from the beginning, the one living and perpetual Church?

And here even antagonists have made great admissions. Chillingworth, a name in the mouths of all men as the first propagator of what is vaunted as the great rule of Protestantism, "the Bible, and the Bible only," that same Chillingworth says that there is a twofold infallibility,—a conditional and an absolute. "The former," namely, a conditional infallibility, he, "together with the Church of England," attributes "to the Church, nay to particular churches." "That is, an authority of determining controversies of faith according to plain and evident Scripture and universal tradition, and infallibility *while they proceed according to this rule.*"* But in whose judgment? In the judgment of the individual? In the judgment of each member of the local and particular church? or in the judgment of the Church Universal? for there can be no other judge to determine whether the particular church moves still in the path of universal tradition. Is the individual

* Chillingworth's Works, vol. i. pp. 276, 277. ed. Oxon.

to be judge of his church? This would be to bid water rise above its source. What then remains? The Universal Church alone can be the judge to pronounce whether or no a local church still keeps within the sphere of universal tradition.

But if this be so, the Universal Church must be infallible; for if it may err, who shall determine whether it errs or no? "Can the blind lead the blind? do they not both fall into the ditch?" It comes, then, by the force of rigorous argument to this, that either the Universal Church cannot err, or that there is on earth no certainty for faith. If, then, the Church Universal be unerring, whence has it this endowment? Not from human discernment, but from Divine guidance; not because man in it is wise, but because God over it is mighty. Though the earth which moves in its orbit may be scarred by storms, or torn by floods; though upon its surface nations may be wasted, cities overthrown, and races perish, yet it keeps ever in its path, because God ordained its steadfast revolutions: so, though individuals may fall from truth, and nations from unity, yet the Catholic Church moves on, because God created it and guides it.

III. And now we must advance one step further. For in dealing with those who are separated from us, I believe that nothing I have yet touched upon really probes the difficulty in their minds. The sore lies deeper still: and it will be found that the reluctance of too many, even among good men, to receive the doctrine of the infallibilty of the Church of God springs from this, that they base their religious opinions upon human reason, either in the individual or upon a large scale, as upon the mere intellectual tradition of Christendom, and not upon the illumination and supernatural guidance of Christ ever present and ever dwelling as a Teacher in the Church. It will be found to involve a doubt as to the office of the third Person of the Ever-Blessed Trinity.

Let us proceed to examine this more closely. We believe that Holy Scripture and the Creeds contain our faith; that for the meaning of these we may not use private interpretation, or wrest them from their divine sense, but must receive them in the sense intended by God when they were given in the beginning. To ascertain that sense, we must go to the Universal Church. Universal tradition we believe to be the supreme interpreter of Scripture. When we come to this point, I ask the objector, Do you believe that this universal tradition of Christendom has been perpetuated by the human reason only? Or do you believe it to be a traditional, divine illumination in the Church? Do you believe that the Holy Spirit, is in the Church; and that His Divine Office is perpetual? If you say that individuals may judge the meaning of Scripture by their own reason: the Church has collective reason, and what the individual has the Church has more abundantly. If individuals are guided by the illumination of the Holy Spirit in the interpretation of Scripture, the Church much more. That which is collective contains all that is individual.

But further than this. "As the sensual man," proceeding, that is, by the natural discernment only, "perceiveth not these things that are of the Spirit of God," because they are "spiritually examined,"* so the Church itself in council depends for its discernment in identifying the original faith, interpreting the original documents, and defining the original truth, on the presence of the Holy Ghost, Whom it invokes at the opening of every session. What is the Church in the mouth of those separated from Catholic unity? Is it more than a human society? Is it not the religious organization of national life? If it be not, like the schools of Athens, collected round the voice of some potent and persuasive teacher, it is at most, like the Jewish people, an organized government of men, as in temporal matters so in ecclesiastical. This is the idea of the Church among those separated from unity. But what do you believe when you speak of the

* 1 Cor. ii. 14.

Church of God? You believe that as the Eternal Father sent the Eternal Son to be incarnate, and as the Eternal Son for thirty-three years dwelt here on earth: as for three years by His public ministry, He preached the kingdom of God in Jerusalem and Judæa, so, before He went away, He said, "I will ask the Father, and He shall give you another Paraclete, that He may abide with you for ever, the Spirit of truth."* The gain we have by His departure is this, that what was then local is now universal; that what was partial then is now in fulness; that when the second Person of the Ever-Blessed Three ascended to the throne of His Father, the third Person of the Holy Trinity descended to dwell here in His stead; that as in Jerusalem the second Person in our manhood visibly taught, so now in the mystical body of Christ the third Person teaches, though invisibly, throughout the world; that the Church is the incorporation of the presence of the Holy Spirit teaching the nations of the earth.

Is not this our meaning when in the Creed before the altar we say, "I believe One Holy Catholic Apostolic Church?" And this touches the point where we differ from those who are without. The discernment they ascribe to the Church is human, proceeds from documents, and is gathered by rea-

* St. John xiv. 16.

soning. We rise above this, and believe that the Holy Spirit of God presides over the Church, illuminates, inhabits, guides, and keeps it; that its voice is the voice of the Holy Spirit Himself; that when the Church speaks, God speaks; that the outward and the inward are one; that the exterior and the interior authority are identified; that what the Church outwardly testifies, the Spirit inwardly teaches; that the Church is the body of Christ, so united to Christ its Head, that he and it are one, as St. Paul declares, "He gave some apostles, and some prophets, and other some evangelists, and other some pastors and doctors, for the perfecting of the saints, for the work of the ministry, for the edifying of the body of Christ; until we all meet into the unity of faith, and of the knowledge of the Son of God, unto a perfect man, unto the measure of the age of the fulness of Christ;"* "from whom the whole body being compacted and fitly joined together by what every joint supplieth, according to the operation in the measure of every part, maketh increase of the body, unto the edifying of itself in charity."

The ultimate authority, then, on which we believe, is the voice of God speaking to us through the Church. We believe, not in the Church, but through it: and through the Church, in God

* Eph. iv. 11, 12, 16.

And now, if this be so, I ask what Church is it that so speaks for God in the world? What Church on earth can claim to be this teacher sent from God? Ask yourselves one or two questions.

What Church but one not only claims, but possesses and puts forth at this hour an universal jurisdiction? What Church is it which is not shut up in a locality or in a nation, nor bounded by a river or by a sea, but interpenetrates wheresoever the name of Christ is known? What Church, as the light of heaven, passes over all, through all, and is in all? What Church claims an universal authority? What one sends missions to the sunrise and to the sunset? What Church has the power of harmonizing its universal jurisdiction, so that there can be no collision when its pastors meet? What Church is there but one before whom kingdoms and states give way? When yet did the Church of Greece, for instance, make a whole nation rise? When did a voice issue from Constantinople before which even a civilized people forgot its civilization? Why came not such a voice from the East? Because there was no Divine mission to speak it.

We are told that all other sects are religions, and may be safely tolerated, but that the Catholic Church is a polity and kingdom, and must therefore be cast out. We accept this distinction. What is this cry but the cry of those who said of old, "We will not have this man to reign over us?" It is the acknowledgment that in the Catholic Church there is a Divine mission and a Divine authority; that we are not content with tracing pictures on the imagination, or leaving outlines on the mere intellect, but that, in the name of God, we command the will; that we claim obedience, because we first submit to it. From the highest pastor to the lowest member of Christ's Church, the first lesson and the first act is submission to the faith of God.

How blind, then, are the statesmen of this world: the Catholic Church an enemy of civil kingdoms! What created modern Europe? What laid the foundations of a new empire when the old had withered in the East? What was the mould from which Christian nations sprang? What power was it that entered into England when it was divided by seven jarring, conflicting kingdoms, and harmonized them as by the operation of light into one empire? What power is it that, as it created all these, shall also survive them all? What created the very constitution of which we are so proud? Whence came its first great principles of freedom? Why do we hear, then, that because the Catholic Church has a polity and is a kingdom, because it claims supremacy, and is found every where supreme, therefore it is not to be tolerated?

It has indeed a power from heaven which admits

no compromise. There is before it this, and this only choice. In dealing with the world, it says: All things of the world are yours; in all things pertaining to you, in all that is temporal, we are submissive; we are your subjects; we love to obey. But within the sphere of the truth of God, within the sphere of the unity and discipline of God's kingdom, there is no choice for the Catholic Church but mastery or martyrdom.

Let us ask another question. What Church but one has ever claimed a primacy over all other Churches instituted by Jesus Christ? Did any Church before the great division, three hundred years ago, save that one Church which still possesses it, ever dream of claiming it? Has any separate body since that time ever dreamed of pretending to such a primacy? Has there ever been in the world any but one body only, which has assumed such a power as derived to it from Jesus Christ?

In answer it is said, "Yes; but the primacy of Rome has been denied from the beginning." Then it has been asserted from the beginning. Tell me that the waves have beaten upon the shore, and I tell you that the shore was there for the waves to beat upon. Tell me that St. Irenæus pleaded with St. Victor, that he would not excommunicate the Asiatic Churches; and I tell you that St. Irenæus thereby recognised the authority of St. Victor to excommunicate. Tell me that Tertullian mocked at the "Pontifex maximus," "the Bishop of Bishops," and I tell you he saw before him a reality that bare these titles. Tell me that St. Cyprian withstood St. Stephen in a point not yet defined by the Church, and I tell you that, nevertheless, in St. Stephen's See, St. Cyprian recognised the chair of Peter, in unity with which he died a martyr. What do wars of succession prove but the inheritance and succession of the crown? What does a process of ejectment prove but that a man is in possession of the disputed property? What truth is there that has not been disputed? Let us apply the argument. Has not the doctrine of the Holy Trinity been denied? Has not the Incarnation been denied? Is there any doctrine that has not been denied? But what is our answer to the Arian and Socinian? Because from the beginning these truths have been denied, *therefore* from the beginning they have been both held and taught.

To go over the field of this argument would be impossible; I will therefore take only one witness of the primacy of the See of Peter. And I will select one, not from a later age, because objectors say, "We acknowledge that through ambition and encroachment this primacy in time grew up;" nor shall he be chosen from the centuries which followed the division of the East and West, because we are told that the exorbitant demands of the West in this very point caused the East to revolt from unity. It shall be a witness whose character and worth, whose writings and life have already received the praise of history. It shall be one taken from the centuries which are believed even by our opponents to be pure,—from the six first centuries, while the Church was still undivided, and, as many are still ready to admit, was infallible, or at least had never erred. It shall be a name known not only in the roll of Saints, but one recognized in Councils, and not in Councils of obscure name, but in one of the four Councils which St. Gregory the Great declared were to him like the four Gospels, and the Anglican Church by law professed to make its rule whereby to judge of heresy. In the Council of Chalcedon, then, was recognised the primacy of St. Leo. Throughout his writings, and especially in his epistles, St. Leo's tone, I may say his very terms, are as follows: "Peter was Prince of our Lord's Apostles. Peter's See was Rome. Peter's successor I am. Peter devolved upon his successors the universal care of all the Churches. My solicitude has no bounds but the whole earth. There is no Church under heaven which is not committed to my paternal care. There is none that the jurisdiction of St. Peter does not govern." We not only hear him claim, but see him exercise acts of jurisdiction in Gaul, in Spain, in

Italy, in Africa, in Greece, in Palestine, and in Constantinople. We find him convening and presiding in Councils; confirming or annulling the canons of those Councils; judging Bishops, deposing and restoring them. Even of Constantinople, the only rival ever put forward to the primacy of Rome, he writes to the Emperor, speaking of the ambition of the Patriarch then in possession: "The nature of secular and of divine things is different, neither shall any fabric be stable but that one rock which the Lord has wondrously laid in the foundation. He loses his own who covets what is another's. Let it suffice for him of whom we have spoken" (*i. e.* the Patriarch of Constantinople), "that by the help of thy piety, and the assent of my favor, he has obtained the episcopate of so great a city. Let him not despise the imperial city, which he cannot make an Apostolic See."* There is no act of primacy exercised at this hour by the Pontiff who now rules the Church which may not be found in its principles in the hands of St. Leo. They who refuse obedience to this primacy must refute St. Leo's claim. Until they do this, they stand in the presence of an authority which no other Church has ever dared to exercise.

We will ask but one question more. What other Church is there that has ever spread itself through all the nations of the world as speaking with the

* S. Leon. ad Marc. Epist. lxxviii.

voice of God? Does Protestantism ever claim in any form to be heard by nations or by individuals as the voice of God? Do any of their assemblies, or conferences, or convocations, put forth their definitions of faith as binding the conscience with the keys of the kingdom of heaven? Do they venture to loose the conscience, as having the power of absolving men? The practical abdication of this claim proves that they have it not. Their hands do not venture to wield a power which in any but hands divinely endowed would be a tyranny as well as a profanation.

And what do we see in this but the fulfilment of a divine example? Of whom is it we read that "the people were in admiration at His doctrine," for this very reason, because "He was teaching them as one having power, and not as their scribes?" He spake not as man, that is, not by conjecture, nor by reasoning, nor by quoting documents, nor by bringing forth histories, but in the name of God, being God Himself. So likewise the Teacher whom He hath sent, comes not with labored disquisitions, not with a multitude of books, not with texts drawn from this passage and from that treatise, but with the voice of God, saying: "This is the Catholic faith, which unless man believe faithfully, he cannot be saved." It comes with the voice of authority appealing to the conscience, leaving argument and

6*

controversy to those who have too much time to save their souls, and speaking to the heart in man, yearning to be saved.

Take Rome from the earth, and where is Christendom? Blot out the science of Catholic theology, and where is faith? Where is the mountain of the Lord's house which Isaias the prophet saw? Where is the stone cut out without hands, which, in the vision of Daniel, grew and filled the whole earth? Where is the kingdom which the God of Heaven hath set up? Where is the "city seated on a mountain" that cannot be hid? If Rome be taken out of Christendom, where are these? I do not ask what churches have laid claim to represent those prophecies. Your own reason says it is impossible. But where, I ask, if not here, is the fulfilment of the words, "Lo, I am with you all days, even unto the consummation of the world?" Where, if not here, is the witness of God now speaking? Where, if not here, is the perpetual presence of the faith of Pentecost?

We stand not before a human teacher when we listen to the Catholic Church. There is One speaking to us, not as scribes and pharisees, but as the voice of God: "He that heareth you heareth Me; and he that despiseth you despiseth Me; and he that despiseth Me despiseth Him that sent Me."*

* St. Luke x. 16.

LECTURE IV.

RATIONALISM THE LEGITIMATE CONSEQUENCE OF PRIVATE JUDGMENT.

St. John xvii. 3.

"This is life everlasting, that they may know Thee, the only true God, and Jesus Christ whom Thou hast sent."

I WOULD fain leave the subject where we broke off in the last lecture. So far as I am able, I have fulfilled the work that I undertook. Hitherto the path that we have trodden has been grateful and onward. We have followed the steps of truth affirmatively; we have been occupied in constructing the foundation and in building up the reasons of our faith. To construct is the true office and work of the Church of God, as of Him from whom it comes. I would fain, therefore, leave the subject here. And yet it is perhaps necessary that we should turn our hand and put to the test what we have hitherto said, by supposing a denial of the truths and principles which we have stated. We began, then, from the first idea of faith; that God, in His mercy to mankind, fallen and in ignorance, again revealed Himself; to the end that through the knowledge of Himself and of His Son incarnate, we might attain life everlasting. We have seen, too, that the very idea of revelation involves the properties of definiteness and certainty, because the knowledge divinely revealed is presented to us as it exists in the mind of God; that, flowing from Him as the only fountain, it descends to us through His Church as the only channel; and that the Church, though universal in its expanse, is absolutely one: a living and lineal body whereby the present is linked with the past, and to-day is united with the day of Pentecost. Wherefore, we do not believe that God spake once, and now speaks no more, but that, beginning to speak then, He speaks still; that what He spake by inspiration when the tongues of fire descended, He speaks yet in the perpetuity of His Church. The teaching of the One, Holy, Universal, Roman Church, the living and present history of the past, is to us the voice of God now, and the foundation of our faith.

Having proceeded, step by step, to this point, it becomes necessary, distasteful as it must be, to turn back, and to undo what we have done: necessary, because truth is often more clearly manifested by contradictories, for in those contradictories we touch at last upon some impossibility, or some absurdity, which refutes itself.

Let it, then, be denied first of all, that the Church whose centre is in Rome, whose circumference is from the sunrise to the sunset—let it be denied that the Church of Rome is the One Universal Church, the Teacher sent from God; and what follows?

No other Church but this interpenetrates in all nations, extends its jurisdiction wheresoever the name of Christ is known, has possessed, or, I will say, has claimed from the beginning, a divine primacy over all other Churches; has taught from the first with the claim to be heard as the Divine Teacher, or speaks now at this hour in all the world. Whatever may be said in theory, no other, as a matter of fact, from the east to the west, from the north to the south, claims to be heard as the voice of God.

Deny this and to what do we come? If we depart from this maximum of evidence, this highest testimony upon earth, to the revelation of God, we must descend to lower levels. Deny the supreme and divine authority of the Universal Church, and in the same moment the world is filled with rival teachers. They spring up in the East and in the West. The East with all its ancient separations,

The West, with all its schisms of later centuries, the Calvinist, the Lutheran, and the Anglican, urge the same demand. Deny the supreme office of this one Teacher, and all others claim equally their privilege to be heard. And why not? It is not for us, indeed, to find arguments in bar of their claim. It is for those who adopt this principle of independence to supply the limitation. We stand secure; but they who, by denying the Catholic rule of faith, introduce these contradictions, are bound to discover the test whereby to know who speaks truth and who speaks falsehood in the conflict of voices.

If fleeing for your life you came to a point where many roads parted, and but one could lead to safety, would it be a little matter not to know into which path to strike? If among many medicines one alone possessed the virtue to heal some mortal sickness, would you be cold and careless to discover to which this precious quality belongs? If Apostles were again on the earth, would you be unconcerned to distinguish them from rivals or deceivers? If there should come again many claiming to be Messiah, would you deem it a matter of indifference to know from among the false Christs which is the true? If one comes saying, "You shall be saved by faith only;" and another, "You shall be saved by faith and pious sentiments;" and another, "You shall be saved by faith without sacraments;" and another,

"There is a divine law of sacramental grace whereby you must partake of the Word made Flesh;" is it a matter of indifference to you to know with certain proof which of all these teachers comes from God? Are we not already in the days of which our Lord forewarns us, that "many shall come in My name, saying, 'I am Christ?'" Is it not of such times as these that the warning runs, "If they shall say to you, Behold He is in the desert, go ye not out,"—that is, to seek the messenger sent from God; "for as lightning cometh out of the east, and appeareth even into the west, so shall also the coming of the Son of Man be?"* The true messenger of God is already abroad in all the earth.

To avoid this impossible theory, a view has been proposed since the rise of the Anglican Church as follows: The Church, it is said, does not consist of those who are condemned for heresy, as the Eutychian, the Monophysite, and the like; neither of those who have committed schism, as the Protestant sects; but it consists of the Greek, the Roman, and the Anglican Churches.

Let me touch this theory with tenderness, for it is still a pleasant illusion in many pious minds. Many have believed it as they believe revelation itself. And if we would have this illusion dispelled, it must be not by rough handling or by derision,

* St. Matt. xxiv. 23-27.

but by the simple demonstration of its impossibility.
If these three bodies, then, be indeed the one Church,
the Church is divided. For the moment pass that
by. If these three be indeed parts of the same
Church, then, as that one Church is guided by one
Spirit, they cannot so far as that guidance extends,
contradict each other. However directly their definitions may be opposed, yet in substance of faith
they must be in agreement. Such are the straits to
which men under stress of argument or of events
are driven. But these three bodies so united in unwilling espousals divorce each other. The Greek
will not accept the Anglican with his mutilation of
sacraments; nor will the Anglican accept the Greek
with his practice of invocation. Neither does the
Holy See accept either with their heresy and their
schism. These three bodies, brought by theory into
unwilling combination, refuse, in fact, to be combined. They can be united only upon paper.

The present relation of the Anglican and Catholic
Churches is a refutation final and by facts of this
arbitrary theory.

The impossibility of this view has compelled many
plain and serious minds to reject altogether the
notion of a visible church, and to take refuge in
the notion of a church invisible. But this too
destroys itself. How shall an invisible church carry
on the revelation of God manifest in the flesh, or

be the representative of the unseen God: the successor of visible apostles, the minister of visible sacraments, the celebrator of visible councils, the administrator of visible laws, and the worshipper in visible sanctuaries? Here is another impossibility to which the stress of argument drives reasonable men.

Abandoning the scheme of an invisible church, others have come to adopt another theory, namely, that the Church of God is indeed a visible body, the great complex mass of Christendom, but that it has no divine authority to propose the faith, no perpetual office, or power to declare with unerring certainty what is the primitive doctrine. They say that during the first six hundred years, while the Church was united, it possessed this office, to decide, and that in the discharge of this office, it was even infallible, or that, at least, it never erred; but that by division it has forfeited the power of exercising this office, that by reunion it may yet one day regain it; and that, in the meantime, every particular church appeals to a general council yet to come. This, too, is believed by some, and with sincerity.

And yet they have never been able to say how it is that a divine office which flows from the Divine Presence should suddenly come to nothing, the Divine Presence still abiding. If, indeed, the third Person of the Holy Trinity dwell in the Church in the stead of the second Person of the Ever-Blessed Three; if the Spirit of truth be come to guide and to preserve the Church in all truth, how is it that the Divine office faithfully fulfilled during six hundred years, in the seventh century began to fail? They turn to the state of the world in ancient times, and say, that as the light of truth possessed before the flood faded until the sin of man brought in the deluge; that as the revelation possessed by Noe decayed until Abram was called out of idolatry; that as the truth revealed by Moses fell into corruption, and the Jewish Church became unfaithful; so the Church of Christ, following the same law of declension, may likewise become corrupt.

But is it possible that men versed in the Scriptures can thus argue from the shadows to the substance; that because in the ancient world, in the old and fallen creation, before as yet the Word was incarnate, or the Holy Ghost yet given; because in those "days of the flesh," men failed and forfeited God's gifts of grace, therefore now, after that the second Person of the Holy Trinity has come on earth in our manhood, and sits at the right hand of God, the glorious Head of His mystical body, upholding by His Godhead the order of grace; that now when the Holy Ghost dwells in His stead as the imperishable life and light of the new creation, the same laws of our fallen nature still prevail, not against men, not against the human element, which no one denies, but against the Divine element and office of the Church? But although every individual man may fail, yet the Church is still infallible; although every man, being defectible, may fall away, yet "the gates of hell shall never prevail against the Church." Although promises to individuals are conditional, yet to the Church, as a Divine creation, they are absolute. Before the Incarnation of the Son of God, the mystical body did not exist. Therefore, in one word, we answer, that the old world has no analogy or precedent to the new creation of God.

Again, it is said that the notes of the Church, sanctity and unity, are to be put in parallel. There are promises we are told, that all the children of God shall be holy, and that every one shall be taught of God. The promises of sanctity, therefore, being absolute, we should have expected a perfect Church without spot or blemish. But we see the visible Church full of scandals and corruptions. Our expectation then in the promise of sanctity not being literally fulfilled, when we read of absolute unity, we ought not to look for a literal fulfilment.

This is an error in which many minds still are held. They forget that unity means one in number, and that sanctity is a moral quality. Again, they do not distinguish between the sanctity which is on God's part, and the sanctity which is on the part of man. The note of sanctity, as it exists on the part of God, consists in the sanctity of the Founder of the Church, the sanctity of the Holy Spirit by whom it is inhabited, the sanctity of its doctrine, and the sanctity of holy Sacraments as the sources of grace. But sanctity on the part of man is the inward quality or state of the heart sanctified by the Holy Ghost. This inward sanctity varies, of necessity, according to the measure and probation of man; but the presence of God the Sanctifier; the power of holy Sacraments, the fountains of sanctification: these divine realities on God's part are changeless; they are ever without spot or blemish, even to the letter of the prophecy. Only the effect upon those who receive them varies according to the faith of the individual. This is the true parallel. The Church is numerically one as God is one. Individuals and nations may fall from unity as from sanctity, but unity, as a Divine institution, stands secure: "The gifts and calling of God are without repentance."[*] Unity is changeless, whoever falls away: it does not admit of degrees. One cannot be more or less than one.

But if, as it is said, the office of the Church to decide questions of faith has been suspended, then

[*] Rom. xi. 29.

the world at this hour has no teacher. Then the command, "Going, therefore, teach ye all nations," is expired. The "nations" mean, not only the nations then dwelling on earth, but the nations in succession, with their lineage and posterity, until the world's end. There is no longer, then, a divine teacher upon earth. If the office of the Church to teach the truth and to detect falsehood, to define the faith and condemn heresy, be suspended, we know not now with certainty what is the true sense even of the Articles of the Creed. Between the East and the West, that is between the universal Roman Church and the local Greek Church, there are two questions open, both of which touch an article of the baptismal faith. One point of doctrine taught by the Catholic Church is this: that the Holy Ghost proceeds both from the Father and from the Son. The Greek Church denies the procession from the Son. Who is right and who is wrong? On which side is the truth in this controversy? Where is the faith and where heresy between the two contending parties? If the office of the Church be suspended, there exists no judge on earth to say who has the truth in this dispute: and that not touching an inferior article of doctrine, but an article of the highest mystery of all, the Ever-Blessed Trinity.

But to take another, and a vital question, namely,

the primacy of the Church itself,—the power that is vested in the See of Peter to control by its jurisdiction all Churches upon earth. In the baptismal faith we profess to believe in one Holy Catholic Church. Surely the question whether or no there be on earth a supreme head of the Church divinely instituted, is as much a part of the substance and exposition of that article as any other point. But yet between the Catholic and the Greek Churches this point is disputed. And if the office of the Church be suspended, there is no power on earth to determine who is right and who is wrong in this contest.

But let us turn from the Greek Church. Let us apply the same tests to the Anglican communion. How many points of doctrine are open between the Anglican and the Universal Church. In the thirty-nine articles of religion, how many points are disputed. How many controverted questions, not with the Roman Church alone, but with the Greek Church also. For instance, the whole doctrine of the Sacraments, their number and their nature, the power of the keys, the practice of invocation, and the like. Then, I ask, if indeed the office of the Church be suspended, who now at this day can declare who is right and who is wrong in these disputed questions?

Nay, we may go yet further, and say, that even

the points of faith decided by Councils when the Church was yet one are no longer safe. There needs only an individual of sufficient intelligence and sufficient influence to rise up and call them in question. If the interpretation of the decrees of the Councils of Nice or Ephesus be disputed, an authoritative exposition of these ancient definitions is required. But this cannot be obtained unless there still sit on earth a judge to decide the law. Suppose a dispute to arise as to the interpretation of a statute passed in the reign of Edward III., and that there were no judges in Westminster to expound it, the law would be an open question, that is, a dead letter. So with the decrees of ancient Councils. It needs, then, nothing but a controversy on each article of the faith to destroy their certainty. Twelve disputes on the twelve Articles of the Baptismal Faith would destroy all certainty. And on earth there would be no judge to say who is right and who is wrong, to declare what was originally revealed on the day of Pentecost, and the meaning of that revelation. To what impossibilities does this theory reduce those who hold it: impossibilities which they perhaps can speak of best who have felt them most. But from this a way of escape is thought to lie in appealing to a future General Council. And yet this brings no present certainty. The faith might be, as in England it is, uncertain for centuries while the General

Council is still future. In truth, this appeal is no more than a plea for insubordination. To appeal from the reigning sovereignty to one to come is simple treason. But besides, the theory is in itself impossible. For who is to convene this future Council? And of whom shall it be composed? Who shall sit in it? Who shall be excluded? And by whose judgment shall the admission and exclusion be determined? Every divided Church will demand its vote and voice. Who shall judge its claim? The office of the judge is in abeyance. But a General Council presupposes the existence and office of the supreme judge of faith and unity. And this the appellants tell us is suspended.

Let us pass on from this point. To deny, then, that the One Universal and Roman Church is now the Teacher sent from God on earth, leads to a denial that there exists in the world any Teacher at all; and to deny the existence of this universal Teacher involves two consequences so impossible, that they need only to be stated to be refuted. If there exists in the world no teacher invested with divine commission to guide all others, either every several local church is invested with a final and supreme authority to determine what is true and what is false; that is, possesses the infallibility denied by objectors to the Universal Church itself;

or else, no authority under heaven respecting divine truth is more than human.

Let us examine this alternative. We may pass by the Greek Church, for it had discernment enough, when it began its schism, to put forward the claim to be not a part of the Church, but the true Church; not to be in communion with others, but to be the sole preserver of the Faith. The Greek Church has at all times claimed to be the temple of the Holy Spirit, and "the orthodox," that is, the only faithful teacher of the truth. It claims also infallibility by guidance of the Holy Ghost. It does not affect to participate with Rome, but to be exclusively the one true Catholic Church. It denounces the Holy See as both in error and in schism. We may then pass over this case, because its very consistency, while it makes the pretensions of the East more unreasonable, confirms our position. We will take a local body which has claimed for itself to be, not exclusively the Church, but a part of it, and within its own sphere to be sufficient to determine controversies, to perpetuate its orders, to confer and to exercise jurisdiction; that is, which has claimed to have within its own sphere all that the Catholic Church possesses from its Divine Founder.

I will not weary you by tracing out historically the theory upon which the highest and most honored names of the Anglican body have attempted to justify the Reformation. It will be sufficient to say that pious and learned men have believed as follows: That in the time of our Saxon ancestors the Catholic Church in this country possessed a freedom of its own; that, though in union with the Holy See, it was under no controlling jurisdiction; that when the Normans came in they established a civil state upon the basis of the existing ecclesiastical order, and therein perpetuated the freedom and privileges of the Catholic Church in England. They further believed that every Christian kingdom, such as ours, had laws, privileges, and rights of its own; and that these among us were usurped upon, interfered with, and taken away by a foreign power, the Bishop of Rome. They taught, then, that the Reformation was nothing but a removal of usurpation and a restoring of our ancient freedom; that the Church which existed before and after the Reformation was one and the same, a continuous and living body, mutilated, indeed, in the wreck of that age, but still preserving its orders, its jurisdiction, and its doctrines; being sufficient in itself to determine all questions, as the notable act of parliament, passed at the beginning of the schism, in its preamble declares.

What was the effect of this theory? It at once invested the local church with all the final prerogatives of the universal. It claimed for it the power within its own sphere to terminate everything that can be terminated only by the Universal Church under Divine guidance. Though it dared not to enunciate the claim, it had practically assumed the possession of infallibility. It would have been too unreasonable and too absurd to state it, but it acted as if it really were infallible. And what were the effects? No sooner did the Anglican Church begin to determine the controversies of its members than they began to dispute its determinations.

The first separation from the Anglican establishment was made by the Independents. They carried their appeal beyond the local church, and because they had been taught to acknowledge upon earth no superior before whom to lay it, they appealed to Scripture and to reason, or, as they thought, to the unseen Head of the Church, but in truth to their own interpretations. The first effect of investing a local body with universal sovereignty in jurisdiction and discipline, was to make truthful and earnest men, who saw the impossibility of such a claim, break out into disobedience. Hence have come the separations from the Anglican Church which now divide England from one end to the other. The source of these divisions is the impossibility of believing that a body formed by private judgment and established by civil power can possess a divine authority to terminate controversies of faith.

We have lately had this theory of local churches tested before our eyes. History told us that in the Anglican Church, during the three hundred years of its existence, there have been two schools of theology, one bearing the appearance of Catholic doctrine and of Catholic tradition; another, earlier in date, springing from the very substance of the Reformation itself, pre-occupying the Anglican communion, a school of pure Protestant theology. These two schools have existed, struggling, conflicting, and denouncing each other from that day to this. Yet it was believed that the Catholic school was the substance of the Anglican Church, and the Protestant a parasite: a malady which, though clinging closely to it, might yet be expelled and cast off.

Such was the belief of many. Then came a crisis. You know, and I will do no more than remind you distantly, how a question touching the first sacrament of the Church, touching, therefore, the first grace of Christian life, original sin, and the whole doctrine of the work of grace in the soul of man—a doctrine fundamental and vital, if any can be—was brought into dispute between a priest and his bishop. The bishop refused to put him in charge with cure of souls. The priest, not content with the decision of his bishop, appealed to the jurisdiction of the archbishop; the archbishop, that is, his court, confirmed the decision of the bishop. The appeal was then further carried to the civil power sitting in council. Observe the steps of this appeal. The bishop here is a spiritual person possessing spiritual authority, sitting as a spiritual judge in a spiritual question. The archbishop to whom the appeal is carried sits likewise as a spiritual judge in a spiritual question, with this only difference, that whereas his jurisdiction is co-extensive with the jurisdiction of the bishop, it is superior to it. When the appeal, then, is carried from the archbishop to the civil power in council, what does that appeal disclose? That the civil power sitting in council sits as a spiritual person to judge in a spiritual question with a jurisdiction likewise co-extensive, and absolutely superior both to bishop and archbishop, an office which in the Church of God is vested in a patriarch. There is no possibility of mistaking this proceeding. It is one of those proofs which are revealed, not in arguments, but in facts.

And now, to what does this reduce the theory of local churches? It shews that local churches possess in themselves no power to determine finally the truth or falsehood of a question of faith. An attempt was made at that time by men, whom I must ever remember with affection and respect, to heal this wound by distinguishing in every such appeal between the temporal element relating to benefice, property, and patronage, and the spiritual element

civil power sitting in council, as the natural judge
that the temporal element should be carried to the
touching the doctrine of faith. It was proposed
in a matter of benefice or temporalities; and that
the spiritual element, or the question of doctrine,
should be carried to the bishops of that local church.
When this proposal was under discussion, these
questions were asked: Suppose that when a question
of doctrine is carried to the united council of the
bishops of that local church, a bare majority of them
should decide one way, and a large minority should
decide the other; will the minds of a people stirred
from the depths, excited by religious controversy,
moved as no other motive in the world can move
them, by dispute on a point of religious opinion—
will they be pacified? will they be assured? will
they hold as a matter of divine faith the decision of
this majority? Again, suppose that mere number
be on the side of the majority, and that theological
learning be on the side of the minority; if the
majority have greater number, the minority will have
greater weight. And will not people adhere to the
few whom they trust rather than to the many whom,
as theologians, they less esteem? And another
question, not asked then, may be asked now by us:
Suppose the whole body of the assembled bishops
f a local church were unanimous, what guarantee
security is there that their decision shall infallibly

be in accordance with the faith of the Church of Christ? A local body has no prerogative of infallibility. If "the Churches of Jerusalem and of Antioch have erred," every local church may err. If these local churches, notwithstanding their antiquity and magnitude, have erred, shall not a body three hundred years old err too? If "General Councils may err," so, much more readily, may a provincial synod. The church which has recorded these assertions has prepared its own sentence. It disclaims an infallible guidance. And if its assembled fathers, with one mind and voice, should declare with unity on any point of doctrine, what security is there that their united decision shall express the faith of the Universal Church? Torn from the Catholic unity, the mind and spirit of the Universal Church has no influx into the Anglican communion. The channel is cut asunder. It has no authority that is more than human, and thereby revealed itself. Some indeed believe that it was a church for three hundred years, and became a schism two years back; that the Anglican position was tenable till then, and has become untenable only since the change was made.

But there is another alternative. The crisis we speak of was either a change or a revelation. They who can look into history and see existing these two schools from the reign of Edward the Sixth, and the supremacy of the crown from the reign of Henry the Eighth; they who can follow the religious contests of England for three centuries, and still say that a change has been lately made for the first time, may say it; but they who believe that the judgment then pronounced by the highest legal authorities in this land was a true and accurate historical criticism of the religious compromise called the Anglican Reformation, will also believe that the issue of the appeal of which I speak was not a change but a revelation of what the Established Church has been from its beginning; that from the first the Anglican communion, though clothed in ecclesiastical aspect, appropriating the organisation of Catholic times, sitting in Catholic cathedrals, professing to wield in its own name Catholic jurisdiction, has never been more than a human society, sprung from human will, with definitions framed by human intellect, possessing no divine authority to bind the conscience or to lay obligations upon the soul.

To deny, then, the authority of the Universal Church as final and sovereign, is to do one of two things: either to invest every local church with infallibility, which is absurd; or to declare that no authority for faith in the world is more than human.

But we must now hasten over one or two other consequences which might well detain us longer.

To deny that there exists for the faith any higher than human authority, is to destroy the objectivity of truth. As the firmament is an object to the eye and as every several light in it is of divine creation; and though all men were blind, the firmament would stand sure, and its lights still shine no less; so the faith is a divine revelation, and every doctrine in it is a divine light; and though all men were unbelieving, the revelation and its lights would shine the same. The objective reality of truth then does not depend on the will or the intellect of man; it has its existence in God, and is proposed to us by the revelation and authority of God. But how can this be, if the basis upon which the truth rests for us be human? Man could not attain to it, else why did God reveal it? Man cannot preserve it, else why did he lose it of old? Men cannot assure it to us, for men contradict each other. Truth never varies, it is always the same, always one and changeless; contradictions spring from the human mind alone. The one fountain of truth is God; the only sure channel of truth is His Church, through which God speaks still. Cancel the perpetual divine authority which brings truth down to us through the successions of time, and what is the consequence? Truth turns into the opinion or imagination of every several man. The polytheism of the ancient world was only the idea of God reproduced in the human understanding after the true knowledge of God was lost. The mind of man which could not exist without the image of God, formed for itself monstrous conceptions of its own. A shifting, moving imagination, ever revolving in its own thoughts, gave forth polytheism. Polytheism was the subjective distortion of truth after its objectivity was obscured.

Let us come to the present time. What are the sects of England but offspring of the subjective working of the human mind, striving to regain the divine idea of the Church as a teacher sent from God? The Reformation destroyed the objective reality of that idea, and the human mind has created it afresh in eccentric forms for itself. In like manner, false doctrines, fanatical extravagances, and perversions of the truth, what are they but struggles of the mind of man to recreate within his own sphere the truths of which the objectivity is lost?

To deny, then, the divine authority of the Universal Church, and thereby to make all authority for faith merely human, is to convert all doctrine into the subjective imagination of each several man. It becomes a kind of waking dream. For what is dreaming but the perpetuity of human thought running on unchecked by waking consciousness, which pins us down to order and rule by fact and by reality? In sleep the mind never rests; it still weaves on its own imaginations. When we sleep perfectly, we are unconscious of what is passing in our minds; when we sleep imperfectly, we say we dream, that is, we remember. When we awake, these visions fly, because matter-of-fact, the eye of our fellow-creatures, common sense, that is, our waking consciousness, brings us back. In like manner, the visible Church, with its rule of faith, its authoritative teaching, its order, its discipline, its worship, is that outer world in which we move. It keeps the spiritual mind in limit and in measure. Dissolve it, and the mind weaves on in its own fancies, throwing off heresies, eccentricities, and falsehood. Let Germany and England be the witness.

Take, for example, the Rationalism of Germany. In its first age, after the Reformation, Lutheranism was rigorously orthodox until it became insufferably dry; and then the soul in man, thirsting for the waters of life, of which it had been robbed, sought to satisfy itself in a sentimental piety, and by recoil cast off orthodoxy as a thing dead and intolerable. This reaction against definite statements of doctrine at a later stage produced the theory that the whole truth may be elicited out of the human consciousness. From whence in the end came two things: one, the theory that sin had no existence; that it is a philosophical disturbance of the general relations of the Creator and the creature; the other, that a historical Christ had never any existence. Such are the results of the subjective states of the human mind when the objective teaching of divine authority is lost.

And now, one more consequence must be noted. When the objectivity of truth is lost, the obligation of law is gone. What is it that binds us by the laws of moral obligation? I pass by the mere laws of nature. I speak now of those higher laws which come from revelation, and I ask, What is it which binds the conscience? The Divine will revealed in those laws. But on what authority are these laws assured to us? and by whom interpreted? Is it by human authority? Can one man bind another by moral obligation to take his view or interpretation of the will or law of God under pain of sin? Can he put forth his view as a term of communion, if communion be a condition of life eternal? Is it possible for a creature to bind his fellow-creatures under pain of sin unless he possess Divine authority to do so? The laws of God do not bind His creatures unless they are made known to them; though, in right, they bind all creatures eternally, yet, in fact, they need revelation to bring home and apply their obligations to the conscience. A doubtful law is not present to the conscience. If a law is uncertain, it is no law to us. It must be clear and definite both in its injunctions and its authority. I ask, then, what is the source of clearness and definiteness in the law and truth of God but the Divine authority of God, not eighteen hundred years ago, but in every century since, in every year, in every day, in every hour, brought home to and in contact with the moral being of each man? Let us take an example. Is it not a law, binding under pain of sin and eternal death, that we should believe the faith? Then no human authority can be the imposer of that law on us. Is it not a law on which we shall inherit eternal life, that we be subject to the authority of God's Church on earth? Then that authority must be divine. Is it not also binding, under pain of sin, that we preserve the unity of the Church? Then the law of unity is a divine law, delivered and applied to us by a present Divine authority.

Let us pass to one more point, and it shall be the last. When the divine authority, the objectivity of truth, and the obligation of law applied to us by that divine authority, are gone, where then, I ask, is revelation? "This is life everlasting, that they may know Thee, the only true God, and Jesus Christ whom Thou hast sent." Hither have we come down, step by step. We have descended as we ascended. We have come down from the highest round of the mystical ladder, at the head of which is the Divine Presence, to the cold ground, barren and bleak, to natural morality and natural society, to human intellect and human conjecture.

We read in prophecy that Antichrist shall come. And in the heated imagination of schismatics and heretics Antichrist has been enthroned in the chair of the Vicar of Christ Himself. But if I look for Antichrist, I look for him by this token, "Every spirit that dissolveth Jesus is not of God, and this is Antichrist."* This, then, is the mark of Antichrist, to deny the Incarnation of the eternal Son; to deny the Revelation of God springing from it; to deny the mystical body of Christ, the universal Church, and the Divine empire of faith. "Every spirit that dissolveth Jesus," every spirit that looseth the bonds of this unity of Jesus; every theory that reduces man from the kingdom of God founded upon the incarnation of His Son, from the guidance of the Holy Ghost, to mere natural society and mere natural reason; this is Antichrist. And if so, where shall we look for it? I look for it where Protestantism has blighted the earth.

And now, finally; when I began I said that I spoke not as a controversialist. I should feel this subject were dishonored, if I were to treat it as a mere argument. Greater things than argument are at stake,—the honor of our Divine Lord and the eternal salvation of souls. How great is the dishonor, of which men think so little; as if truth were a sort of coin, that they may stamp and change, and

* 1 St. John iv. 3.

vary its die and fix its value, and make it in metal or paper as they will! They treat the truth as one of the elements of human barter, or as an indulgence which a man may hold and use for himself alone, leaving his neighbor to perish. "This is truth to me; look you to what you believe." What dishonor is this to the person of our Lord! Picture to yourselves this night upon your knees the throne of the Son of God; cherubim and seraphim adoring the glory of Eternal Truth, the changeless light of the Incarnate Word, "yesterday, to-day, and for ever the same;" the heavenly court replenished with the illumination of God; the glorified intelligences, in whose pure spirit the thought of falsehood is hateful as the thought of sin;—then look to earth on those whom the blood of Christ hath redeemed; look on those who in this world should have inherited the faith; look at their controversies, their disputes, their doubts, their misery; and in the midst of all these wandering, sinning, perishing souls, look at those who stand by in selfish, cold complacency, wrapping themselves in their own opinion, and saying, This is truth to me.

Think too of the souls that perish. How many are brought into the very gulf of eternal death through uncertainty! How, as every pastor can tell you, souls are torn from the hand which would save them by being sedulously taught that the deadliest sins have no sin in them; by the specious and poisonous insinuation that sin has no moral quality; how souls have first been sapped in their faith as Satan began in Paradise, "Yea, hath God said?" that is, God hath not said. This is perpetually at this hour going on around us; and whence comes it? Because men have cast down the divine authority, and have substituted in its place the authority of men, that is, of each man for himself.

And now, what shall I say of England, our own land, which a Catholic loves next to the kingdom of his Lord? It is now in the splendor and majesty of its dizzy height, all the more perilous because so suddenly exalted. What is the greatness of England? Is it founded on Divine truth, or on human strength and will? Is it material, or is it moral? Has it attained this mighty altitude among nations by the power of moral elevation, or is it the upgrowth of mere material strength? Let us analyse it. What is it that makes England great in the world? Colonies which fill the earth. What are the morals of those colonies? How were they won, how have they been kept? Armies. What are the morals of armies? Fleets. What are the morals of fleets? Commerce. What is the morality of traders? Wealth. "The desire of money is the root of all evils." Manufacture. What is the state of our mines and factories? And whence comes the industry of England? The nerve, the sinew, the strength, and the perseverance are moral; but what is the purity, the truth, the meekness, and the faith of those who wield this industry? And whence comes this mighty power of manufacture? Shall I not trace it to its one true source if I find it in the skill of applying science to subdue the powers of nature to the dominion of man? The mighty bubble of wealth, commerce, and splendor, may be traced back to this: that the skill of an intellect and the tact of a hand have taught the English people more cunningly than any nation of the world to apply physical and mathematical science to the production of material results. But where is the morality of this? I deny not to England great moral qualities, which we may also trace back to Catholic days. We see them in times past, in the Norman and the Saxon ages. Nay, we may go further. We may find the same love of truth and social order, with other great moral laws, in the German race, as described in Pagan history. We deny not these; but moral virtues which existed before faith are not the fruits of faith; and the greatness of England, so far as I have traced it, is material and not moral.

And now, last of all, let me ask another question. What, for three centuries, has been the history of the Faith in England? I pass over the controversy of the Reformation, first, because we are of one mind about it, and next, because it would but beg the question of an objector. I would ask, Is it not an undeniable historical fact, that from the time of Queen Elizabeth down to the time of the revolution of William the Third, there was a perpetual diminution of belief in England, and a perpetual growth of infidelity and scepticism, until, after 1688, the free-thinking philosophy formed for itself a literature that stood high in the public favor of England? The Established Church had wasted itself by internal conflicts. It lost its most zealous members by perpetual secession and by the formation of a multitude of sects. Though the Prayer-book and the Articles were unchanged, the living voice of the Church, that is, its true doctrine, varied continually from doctrinal puritanism to Arminian Anglicanism. The clergy spent themselves in domestic controversy; while the laity became worldly, latitudinarian, and unbelieving. And yet it was not from among the laity, but from among the clergy and the hierarchy, that the hardly concealed Socinianism of Hoadly arose and spread in force. Such was the internal state of the Establishment. Without and around it the doctrine of faith decayed faster and deeper. Doctrine after doctrine was disputed and gave way; the doctrine of Sacraments, of the Atonement, and of inspiration, perpetually lost ground, until we descend to the level of the Deist in the beginning of the last century. Can these facts be denied? The course of England was downward in faith, because human authority, in the stead of divine, had enthroned itself in the Reformation. That which in Germany produced pure Rationalism, in England, but for the interposition of God, would have produced the same general unbelief of Christianity.

Then began a reaction. Take the history of the last century and of the present, and tell me whether I do not truly describe the intellectual progress of England when I say that there has been one continuous and ascending controversy from the beginning of the last century to this hour? First, it was a controversy against Deists, to establish the fact of revelation. Next it was a controversy against sceptics, to prove the inspiration and authenticity of Holy Scripture. Then it was against Arians in proof of the doctrine of the Holy Trinity. Then it was against Socinians on the doctrine of the Incarnation. Then the controversy of the day was on the doctrines of grace. At a later period of the last century it was on the doctrines of conversion, repentance, contrition, the interior life of God in the soul of man. What has been the controv of the last twenty years but an effort to restor in the Divine institution and supernatural gr Sacraments? What is all this but the remn faith struggling to recover the inheritance it had lost? And what has come now to put a complement and close to this upward movement? Now, when the mere human origin and authority of all other teachers has been revealed by their visible departure from the faith, comes one truth more to fill up the order and series of our Baptismal Creed, and to give Divine certainty to all that had been re-established. The Divine authority of the Universal Church has again reconstituted its visible witness in this land. The See of Peter has restored what our fathers forfeited; and after three hundred years the Divine Voice speaks to faith through the Catholic Episcopate of England once more.

Are these things without a purpose? If there be any here who is still without the Divine tradition of the faith, let him see in these facts the tracings of the finger of God, which, as the hand of a man upon the wall, shew His purpose. The Divine authority of the Universal Church is again among us, and lays again its obligation upon your conscience. He calls you, whoever you be, to submit to his teaching, to exercise the most reasonable act of all your life, to bow your reason to a Divine teacher, and to fulfil the highest act of the human intelligence—to learn of its Maker.

Out of the Catholic Church two things cannot be found, reality and certainty; in the Catholic

Church these two things are your inheritance. Then tarry no longer. "With the heart we believe." It is not a struggle of the intellect, and I am not contending with you in an intellectual contest. I call upon your will to make an act of faith. Preventing grace illuminates the understanding, and there tarries. It tarries that it may put man on his probation, to see whether he will correspond or no to the light that has been granted. Correspond, then, with the light you have received. Answer while yet you may: "Speak, Lord, for Thy servant heareth. My heart is ready. Not Thy truth fails, but my faith is weak. I do believe, Lord: help my unbelief."

THE END.

www.ingramcontent.com/pod-product-compliance
Lightning Source LLC
Chambersburg PA
CBHW020900160426
43192CB00007B/1003